Between Dusk and Night

Between Dusk and Night

Emily McGiffin

Brick Books

Library and Archives Canada Cataloguing in Publication

McGiffin, Emily, 1980-
      Between dusk and night / Emily McGiffin.

Poems.
ISBN 978-1-926829-73-9

      I. Title.

PS8625.G52B48 2012   C811'.6   C2011-908123-7

We acknowledge the Canada Council for the Arts, the Government of
Canada through the Canada Book Fund, and the Ontario Arts Council
for their support of our publishing program.

The cover image is a photograph of Hudson Bay Mountain by Brian Huntington.

Cover design by Cheryl Dipede.

The author photo was taken by Dany Couture.

The book is set in Centaur.

Design and layout by Alan Siu.

Printed and bound by Sunville Printco Inc.

Brick Books
431 Boler Road, Box 20081
London, Ontario N6K 4G6

www.brickbooks.ca

for Connie and Eleanor

Contents

Wokkpash

Dusk. On all sides
mountains

walk into blue distance
without pause, without sound—

four days
and you have seen no one.

Here in this gloaming, this coyote
light thick with the unnamed,

instinctive, earthy, you know nothing
the dusk doesn't. And how uneasy:

at the treeline, even
traces of your kind disappear;

the route's just creek bed
and caribou tracks through the pass.

From the folding summer, night
draws its old breadth,

restless. This shifty air and silence
gnaw at your hands

with that old wish
to have done better. And the dying

asters, the fireweed
blazing seed, the grey and fossil-scarred scree,

it all could have
tried harder. Maybe

next year, still
only a thought—

but there is no one
here. Tomorrow does not exist.

Or else lies somewhere
in the time it takes a leaf to fall,

for an arête to become a plain,
that time only

a measure of forgetfulness
more vast than this quiet mountain

sky
and its brief bloom of stars.

It doesn't matter. In the half-dark,
in this wolfish light, you are cold

awake with everything thoughtless,
everything without cause,

without reason. You crouch there
crepuscular,

animal,
alive.

Setting Out

The day she leaves the Whittaker Farm, she will butcher
the last six chickens and drown the cat. All morning
the iron reek of viscera will tarnish the sticky
late summer air. She will pack everything she owns
into a suitcase and an old feed sack, reflecting
that she has never before made such a clean
break—and wondering if it will become habit.

Tumbler

$500 car. Defunct stereo. Long dirt road,
foot hard on the gas, summer landscape
a cappella—the volume cranked. Rock
and spruce shoot past in the rosy flush
of the long last light and you can't eat
the kilometres fast enough. Then a dip and a rise and the sudden
ramparts of the mountain landscape erupt from the forest.
"Vast"? Inadequate. It thumps the wind out. The heart
flutteringly aware of how paltry it is,
how very much larger it must become, that it must
pull over, abandon the car, clamber up the talus verge to the edge
of evening, edge of the land galloping
farther into roadless dusk than the fading light can reach
and stand there, watching night pivot on its hinge
like an old trunk's satin-lined lid; watching for that instant
when the alpenglow flares up the piebald eastern peaks,
that last flourish when everything yet to come – the heavy work
your shoulders want; the imprint your waking body
leaves behind it in the grass; the way someone's face, gladdened,
will unlatch and open for you—
everything lies ahead: a long shadow
dissolving into the larger dark.

Another Summer

Everything left out—books and letters,
the hammock, all the laundry in the alders—soaked in a deep-summer rain,
the spirea thunderheads piled on the seared-air,

                  damp-dust,

                        seed-pod

smell of late August quick-doused in its burning down to tinder fall. Broke
inside and out, I live in my car. Rain on the roof like buckets of nails
dropped. The windows weep as though nothing
will ever be dry again.

These days I would so gladly return to what was, briefly, home:
five a.m. coffee, redpolls in the aspen, Lao Tzu
and my own slow breath.

One thing falls into another—though any sort of
alignment is only ever the mind's work.
Crouched in the damp car, I lay out
hand after hand of solitaire.

Rain

All that I can write: sad lines
trickling down the windshield
of a broken-down car
that's altogether more reliable
than any of my promises. I have none
of the proper words, only
the handfuls of damp twigs
one might try half-heartedly to set alight
when there's no better tinder around.

As Air

If you could know how I crave
weightlessness,

the state that is almost
non-existence.

How often I look back
for the moment my footprints
fade from sight

the dew undisturbed and the moss—
the point when I finally take

       nothing.

And so I empty
the air of me;
it presses in sweet as a small hand,
       intimate as skin.

And as the architecture of my bones
surfaces like a lost city
       I wish you could see

the true weight of our presence here;
       how much soft green light
       my shadow swallows whole.

Parasitism

Coming back through the long grass at the lakes
what worries us most—though of course
no one wants to be the one to mention it—
is the thought of a tick
creeping through the foils of our clothing unnoticed
into the warm folds of labia or scrotum. The thought of its head
buried in private utopia up to its thick black shoulders, its body
gorged and grey, swollen to the size of a dime, inadequate feet braced
against our most intimate parts. More than beasts, more
than any tooth or claw, it's this insidious trespass that most disturbs—
though we might admire, aversely, such recalcitrance, we do not love it.

Instead the loveliness we cleave to
in our mountains, grasses, lakes
is not unruly but deferential: reliant
on our goodness: measured and wary.

Rainstorm

The law, in its majestic equality, forbids the rich as well as the poor
to sleep under bridges, to beg in the streets or to steal bread.
~Anatole France

Wet placards and warrior slogans. The rain, in its majesty,
drenches the high-rises and the panhandlers too.
Talk politics these days and your tongue swells. A boycott
on oranges again, chocolate, sugar. Life
gets harder the more you know. Time to chalk it all up
to inescapable natural law: everything looks out for its own
interests. You're just allelopathic enough
to clear a bit of space to live in and shop
for a clean house with indoor plumbing. Living
is a temporary momentum, brief assemblage of order until all potential energy
is devoured by kinetic: the long column of you toppling, slipped vertebrae
laid out pocked and greying in the sun.
It's just easier
when pine means
shelving. Air freshener. Unrequited
love. Not the long haul of time and ashes
as the slim green progeny of ancients extend
amid the tusks of their dead and bleached forebears
with no concept of all history's clutter under their feet, only patience
and a long unfolding
under the benevolent rain.

Anaemia

The first blood you took
was that of a woman, eight months pregnant,
on methadone. You peered into the scarred
crook of her elbow as she steadied your hand.
Nah, not that one. Too deep. And that one's tricky:
always rolls away. Yeah, good one...Damn,
she bent closer, *that is a good one!*
You tell me this years after the cramped clinic
with its mingled scents of antiseptic and booze,
still struck by that tough intimacy
with her own tempered veins.

Anaemic, my blood
snakes through bone scaffolds
into a vial—warm, still breathing.
A small abduction for far-off strangers
who read the minute language
of erythrocytes and know me
by type, haemoglobin count,
age and the name of my condition.

I couldn't ask you to stay. Again
there is no cure for this affliction
of partings and absences. I wish
there were more iron in me!
I want veins strong as rebar,
or at least lignin: rooted
in ground we could call home.

Una via dove mi specchio

Whoever is alone will stay alone,
will sit, read, write long letters through the evening,
and wander the boulevards, up and down,
restlessly, while the dry leaves are blowing.
~Rainer Maria Rilke

After all this time, what can I tell you
but that autumn is an elegy,
a funereal chant through a fog
of incense, sepulchre for the verdant bust
of an old friend I love too much but forget
easily. Along the boulevards, misty

sycamores drip like rusting pipes and missing
bits of you drift in on the wind chimes. Autumn letters to you
were always of a certain persuasion, *e.g.* on his last day, Gaudí forgot
the traffic as he left the Sagrada Família. Elegiac:
he was struck by a bus.
In fall, under a concealing fog,

this is all too common. For instance: a fogged-
up Greyhound. Westbound. Night. The misted
window streaked with flirtations: *Pacific*, we wrote, *or bust*—
backwards, of course, then fumbled with zippers. You,
unfortunately, weren't there. Later, I wrote you an elegy:
So much time passes. Some things are just hard to forget.

After all this time, you've probably forgotten
how we sat drinking refosco that foggy
night on the terrace of the trattoria. The first elegy:
the night I realized that, despite all your missing
affection, I was smitten. I should have told you,
saved the postage. What good letters I wrote! Like a busted

LP. Or an armaments factory, forging robust
epistles to avenge the shot-through heart. I forget
how much refosco I bled. Now, like others, you
exist in past tense, and my sketch of you on the landscape fogs
over. But in the leaden autumn, sadness will never go missing:
everywhere it floats. Nothing is as buoyant as an elegy.

November. Fog slinks by in mourning; an elegy
in grey. I'm on a street corner staring after a bus—
the same one I missed
yesterday. I've been reading Saba; I'd forgotten
most of your city but the colour of its stones—opal as fog—
and the wind in the plane trees under your

window. And autumn is an elegy. Even after all this trying to forget.
So I'll bust out the rye whiskey and tell the bitter fog:
just six months 'til we see sun again. That, and: I miss you.

Note on Astronomy

Under a salted black sky
you peer into the throng of stars—*Orion!*

It's what we've hoped for:
a means of converting the deep cold dark
to a friendly giant. Orion to bring home
a fattened fall bear so that we can sit together
all winter on a black rug, chewing jerky in the smoky tallow light.

Caught out in bleak November, we've been looking
for bona fide companions. Or a mathematical
equation. For irrefutable signposts on a well-marked path
to trot down blithely, knowing at last how to proceed,
how to slip beyond the confines of our scanty minds
into the real meaning of things.

The fog rolls in off the lake. And I cannot help but hope
that a plant deprived of sun will grow on anyway, blindly, bent
on a half-remembered promise. That in this same gesture
of pure desire, dandelions burst through pavement, lichen
devours a skyscraper, saxifrage—minutely, mutely—
in silence dismantles a wall.

Living at 9.8 m/s^2

At the top of Mount Tzouhalem we toss pebbles
off the cliffs. It is one of those raw moments of early spring sunlight
wrapped around something half-perceived
rushing through us faster
than we can carry our slowing feet up here. Not love.
Not grief, not anything human. Something that makes us look backward
over our shoulders to the deep trees as we fling pebbles
at the darker firs below, the light lulling us
into laziness while the stones, falling
through their brief arc of empty blue, accelerate.
There is an equation for the parabola
we throw across the sky. We could count the seconds of each drop
and, knowing certain velocities, angles,
find the height of these cliffs—but what matters
is the whistle of that falling: the wind in our ears now,
gathering speed.

Dioskorides

He names each land for what grows there:
Nardos. Kyklaminos.
That is how he cloaks geology
in his own tongue: the surest way
to tame distance.

At the oars, a game to pass the time:
they list ruined cities, islands,
villages left behind.
When he replies unthinking,
his companion grins.
That is not a city. That's a plant.

Later, leaning together on the rail,
they translate the coast for one another,
Latinus tracing the line of near hills,
smooth and brown and smelling of sun,
as he tells their stories and those of the winds:
each painting the sea a different blue.

Dioskorides speaks of the iris plant,
roots beneath knotty and strong.
How to dig these and dry them in the shade
hanging from a linen cord. The best
are from Illyria, Macedonia. Of these,
the best again are thick and yellow, bitter.
They are warming, bring sleep,
provoke tears. He falls silent.

Later again, rolling to lie facing the stars,
he wills the plants to grow beneath his eyelids,
to blossom white in the cool shadows

near the azure lake of his youth,
June bugs roaming lazily over the petals.

Hours pass. He knows no remedy
for this smell of blood
he cannot wash from his hands,
for the dark birds circling his mind
above the broken flesh, the splintered bones
that no amount of herbage will repair.

Cave Paintings

I

That afternoon, as we lay in the sea hunting animal shapes in the clouds,
you looked beyond the waves and saw the phantom island. At last
a sure way out (or back)! We splashed to shore laughing
and gazed across the hazy distance, our hands raised
against the glare and the beating sun—until dusk
fell and left us crouched
in the buzz of a fly-battered street light
staring at the wall of night.

II

Twelve thousand years and the painting is still there:
a row of blind figures stooped in orison
under the thumbprint stars
await a child with a torch to stare out, ashen and alone.
The flame wavers and he calls to his companion—
but here's no answer save an echo
as his voice fades into the rock.

Altar

At dusk we gather with the others to pray.
I carry the goat across my shoulders;
Spike brings a joint and a bottle of gin.
But when we reach the shrine above the parking lot
all our silk flowers are gone and some jerk
has kicked in the screen! We all just stand there
as Maria plays a few chords on the squeezebox
and the goat gets loose—takes off into the trees.
Nobody's brought a watch or even a light
and we've forgotten what we're s'pposed to do next.

Cuttlefish Bone

Non domandarci la formula che mondi possa aprirti...
~Eugenio Montale

i.

After the typhoon, the Thu Bon River rose
and prowled the streets, lifting things
while people slept and carrying them away.
Forget sandbagging. Instead people moved furniture
to the upper storeys of their houses or, if they were too poor
for upper storeys, to the roof. Neighbours
sat up there together, sipping tea on the tiles
as they watched fishermen in dugout canoes
ply the streets below. It was like some absurd
party game, the way everyone seemed to smile and laugh,
splashing around in water that gulped at their waists.

(Had you ever been so completely
parenthetical? You and a handful of stranded
tourists. Invisible; disoriented by crowds,
the unending babel of voices.)

ii.

Lines of beach chairs and bamboo huts
abandoned to the grey, insistent, mediocre wind.
A dark woman in a red sweater sits beside you on the ground.
That handful of words in common: exhausted.
So she rises and goes back to raking the sand
and already you're travelling in your mind
to more cheerful places: the comfortable guest house,
the pagoda courtyard where small blue fish
circle their clay pot while a monk in thick glasses
and his supplicants chant in the dim room beyond.
There you can unfurl like morning glory
and trumpet your peace to the Buddhas.

But now a man has pulled a large fish from the waves
and the woman joins the others gathered to admire it
drowning in its nightmare of light.
Trash roams by in the wind and a couple of stray dogs
nip each other, pawing at the sand. No one sees you
lift your bicycle and pedal up the path between the palms.

iii.

The beach again, further on, late afternoon under a stony sky.
Three of you here: an old woman, ragged, her teeth stained black
carries a sack of trash; a boy with a net runs like a sandpiper
in and out of the waves. The beach: a silver bracelet
half buried in the sea, tarnished ash grey, gem-studded
with light bulbs, bleach bottles, Styrofoam, shoes.
The woman disappears over the dune. The boy, luckless,
tosses and tosses his net. You, with the soft hands, you stand in the sea
that surges like tar around your ankles, the spume clotting sepia
on the sand. East and west, the strand
dwindles into distance. How long will you stand here idly
lulled by wave chant, lost
in the white noise of your mind?

Saint-Rémy-de-Provence

Consider a garden of blue irises—

how there are never only irises,
but always irises and *Les Iris:* Van Gogh's
flourish of oils alive amid the blossoms,
just as they are always there, blue and real,
behind his paint or in it.

In a wheat field flecked with poppies—
where a parched wind licks the grain yellow—
I am in a landscape far out of view:
a ceiling of spruce, the ocean
pummelling a grey slate shore. It is here
under the cypresses, in the ferny sandstone
housing of a well: that true home.

And because Picasso and the rest of us
have seen a violin, what he paints
abandons the expected form; his lines
are warbler's trill, the maple, its curlicue shavings,
the composer, intent, drawing sheet music
out of the pulse of his mind. Yet we find it

every time: the shape we want
and know too well—nothing in his geometry
but the violin again, its silhouette
embossed in our skulls.

Thus in a Provençal field: the desired
                              (pines
on a mountainside alive with rain
in spring, the snow just gone, everything drowned
in the howl of wind) slipping
into the real
                    (flesh
and paint in that moment before
memory: buckled old hands
on a watering can; the face of a statue
softened away by rain).

Afternoon of Your Parting

In the shadowed window of a café on Pier Street,
halving our way through the last bite of some excessive
chocolate dessert, I read you a piece about glass-blowers,

how their art is a variant of absence:
coloured spheres a tempered striving
to catch breath's flight, sunlight falling through.

An extension, I guess, of our human physiology:
the heart healing around an emptiness
into some tougher, brighter thing.

Insects in Lamplight after Rain

Sundays on Spark Road begin like this: first the crackling blare of the muezzin parades through the velvet dark. Then footsteps, voices. Slowly, silhouettes take shape as the darkness eases back. The boy from across the dirt street unlocks the wellhead, pulls off the chain and the pump outside creaks into service, children clamouring around it as the daylight grows. At seven a.m., the sky swings abruptly from dawn into full, brassy day and as the air thickens with dust and heat, amplified sound checks burst from the bamboo church next door. An hour later the service kicks off: djembe drums and rattles take off at a gallop with a chorus of lusty *hallelujahs* sashaying along behind.

This particular Sunday, as drums and singing give way to the evangelical zeal of a preacher making full use of his hefty amp, I sit waiting in the shade of a mango tree on the concrete steps of the compound. Abdul is late, and though I should have anticipated it I can't seem to get over expecting things to happen on time.

"All FLESH is GRASS!" bellows the preacher, "ALL FLESH is grass!" He pauses: "GRASS!! "

I pick my nails and stare at the stubborn papaya tree rooted on a boulder behind the church until at last the crunch of gravel announces Abdul's arrival.

"Yeah, let's go."

Leaning against the boulder, he jerks his thumb toward the road. I lift the backpack I've filled with bottles of water, hot-weather gear and some bread and tinned sardines for lunch and follow him into the searing mid-morning sun.

He leads me down Spark Road, beneath mango trees laden with green fruit, through the shambles of burned-out cinder-block houses with their makeshift roofing of rice sacks and rusted tin and faded tarps left by the UNHCR. The road dips into a gully lush with gardens where pale egrets stand amid okra, and women in bright coloured wraps straighten to watch us pass. Nearby, a man tills a field with a mattock. There are no cars on the road, just walkers, the occasional motorbike, sometimes two Limbe men jogging together towards town, each with a stick across his shoulders, a ten-gallon jug of palm wine hung from each end. We round a corner where a band of children spot us and run shrieking to the edge of the road.

"White-ooman! White-ooman!"

They gather at a safe distance and stand giggling in their torn, too-big clothes, pointing, poised to bolt.

"White-ooman!"

We pass the boarded-up building that was the Arabic school where Abdul went as a child—only one year because there were too many other things to do.

"Like what?"

"Helping my mother," he says. "There was a lot of work. Making the garden, making the food. Bringing water, water, water. We lived in the village then. The school was *far!*"

Through that morning, out of the trees, into the heat of the tarnished noonday sun. Past banana sellers and groundnut sellers, through sleepy villages where old men call greetings from the dark verandas of their red mud-brick homes. At Masundu we leave the main road and cross a seeping brook onto the web of footpaths that thread through the savannah into the hills. He begins to greet people in his own language, a string of salutations and replies repeated like a mantra as they pass us with scarcely a glance and carry on down the path.

Our acquaintance began over tea one day when a friend guided me to Abdul's shop after work. I sat on a low bench at the edge of the tea shop that gradually filled with diamond miners gathering for a bit of company at the end of the day. Outside, ex-combatant taxi drivers roared up and down the main street on motorbikes bartered from the UN with arms. Abdul sat beside me and we chinked the awkward silence with brief questions and replies.

Many days and many cups of powerful sweet tea later, he tells me that his brother Ismael mines diamonds, too, and after this things change. Now each time I leave Koidu by the main road I look out at the miners toiling in their vast mud landscape of pits and tailings and wonder if Ismael is among them. Maybe that one, leaning into his spade to heave a dripping mass of red soil out of the soup of his work. The woman who washes clothes near him, perhaps that is his wife, the child splashing beside her would be Abdul's nephew. The town has shrunk. Now only a maybe lies between him and everyone else I meet.

Like the man I'd seen making his way through the streets with the help of a small boy and a stick. One afternoon he stopped at the shop. Thin as a pestle, his eyes clouded over, he stood in the sunshine beyond the curb and smiled confidently into the gloom under the zinc. I noted him idly and looked back toward the din of the street until I saw Abdul step out to place something wordlessly into his hand. The beggar took both Abdul's hands, smiled more broadly, and slid the banknote into his pocket.

After a couple of weeks, Abdul visits one evening with a deck of cards and a small silver radio in his shirt pocket. We slap cards on the table and mosquitoes off our ankles as the BBC World Service crackles out the latest riots, wars and general chaos beyond our small circle of lamplight. Fuel prices go up and up. In Senegal, they riot over the cost of rice. I shuffle and deal the cards while a multitude of spindly, translucent creatures gathers to pay homage to the lamp.

It is quiet tonight, but the rains have begun. Nights when he lies on the floor of his shop listening to rain thunder down on the zinc, Abdul listens also for the small rustling of thieves who will pour acid on an unguarded lock and slip inside. Yesterday, the merchant three doors down was robbed, the rain drowning all but the nearest sounds. He tells me this without the smallest trace of self-pity: goods must be guarded if one is to run a shop, so he spreads a reed mat on the concrete behind a rusty steel door amid criminals who roam the night streets with pry bars and bottles of acid.

"Very wicked boys," he says, laying down a king. Then he gazes up at me: "Hungry boys."

I look down at my cards. I'd been building a Royal Flush but all along we've been playing Go Fish.

By eleven o'clock Abdul is the victor of ten games in a row. He turns off the radio, smirking, and slides it back into his pocket. The night watchman nods as he strides onto the dark road back down to his shop. I blow out the lamp. The sound of frogs fills a darkness interrupted only by the tip of the watchman's cigarette.

Half an hour on the trails and we begin to see cattle. Soon after that the first cluster of round, palm-thatched huts pulls into view. We approach it slowly, watching for bulls, then step through the shrubbery into a packed earth yard. A small man in a faded blue agbada and fitted cap, his lean dark face all canyons of lines, steps forward in greeting.

Abdul says a few words and the man's face opens in happiness. He places his hand on Abdul's shoulder and addresses me, thumping his chest. "My uncle," explains Abdul. The man is delighted and the two stand talking while I scratch the ears of a curious goat. At length he points us toward the furthest hut and returns to tending his cattle.

Abdul was twelve when he fled to Guinea. The rebels screamed in with guns and machetes and he ran with his family out of the village and on toward the border. Everyone from those villages fled, clutching a few meagre belongings and the hands of small children in the terrifying dark. The wind passed over and they were gone. They are still gone, the soft folds of the hills too full of sorrow to return. He tells me now, as we leave his uncle and walk towards the hut, that this is his first journey back.

Neneh is standing with her back to us pounding cassava in a mortar. When Abdul speaks her name she turns slowly and stands very still with her hand on the pestle, looking at him. A slight breeze comes up and rocks the palm trees languidly overhead. She is old, though likely younger than she looks, weather-beaten and wiry. She stands silently, regarding us, a long sigh of unreadable emotions falling across her face. He tells me later that this sight of him was also the sight of his mother, his brothers. For a moment he has carried the village back with him.

She turns and gestures us through a low doorway into the single room of the small round hut that she's just painted with a fresh layer of dung. Two small boys creep in after us and crouch in the shadows, watching. Abdul pulls open his backpack and I see with surprise that all this way, through the heavy equatorial heat, he's carried three large bags of salt. Now he takes them out and places them carefully side by side on the floor of the hut. Neneh watches in silence and when he has finished she looks up and thanks him. She stows the bags one by one in an enamel basin and stacks it against the wall. Then she serves us a dish of fermented milk from another basin and we sit eating, looking out at the afternoon sunlight draped over the long-horned cattle and the gentle hills beyond. I have nothing to say but *hello* and *thank you*, but nothing much is said anyway. We sit keeping company and after some time Abdul rises and ducks back out into the yard. I follow, blinking in the sudden light, and Neneh comes behind, sending one of the boys running off behind the hut. He returns with a small brown hen. Neneh ties its feet together with a strip of rag, hands it to me and smiles.

The shabby boys stand barefoot in the dust, grinning up at me earnestly as I take their gift. A gift the equivalent of what? three days? a week's pay? Their skinny little boy bodies are so frail, riddled with God knows what parasites. I look away. I can feel the chicken's startled heart beating against its ribs.

I say slowly, Neneh, this war-besotted place! This place of sickness and sadness and the squalor of poverty. This place knows a dignity and grace that leaves me shamefaced. Again and again, this silent passage of a few coins, a morsel of food from one impoverished hand to another. That calm, pious gesture that knows suffering and answers it. I say to her, Neneh, I thought I knew how to be good!

She is still smiling at me, the hen clucking softly in my arms.

No, what I say to her is this: "*Jaramah buoi*, Neneh." Thank you so much.

After a Journey

There is a language roots write through the soil;
you've begun to learn it, pressing your ear
night after night to the earth
until their words are almost of your body
after so much conspiring with your sleeping bones.

Now you are thinking of your footfalls in a forest
becoming sure as your heartbeat, as rain—
you grow so still a thrush
lights on your wrist, forgetting
to be afraid. And near you a beetle
emerges from under a leaf;
it has found the sun and remembers
its own limbs, its stiff grace.
What it must do.

Breakwater

August. The air thick with heat. A hot tar
silence on everything, the house
steeped in it. All morning
the cat has been strange and you've been
strange too and it's some hours now
that you've been out. This
is one of those times we've hidden

all the sharp objects. One
of those times I've lost the words
for everyday things (affection, quiet)—
they've become hostile, unrecognizable.
And my mute, illiterate heart gropes
its way after you down the unlit tunnel
of your sadness. And that icy waterfall
sorrow falls onto us, thunderous.
Even alone now, checking my watch,
its omniscient roar floods
the thick creosote heat.

And I go out too quickly, fumbling
for my sunglasses, my shoes.
It's foolish to think of finding you,
yet there you are three blocks away,
walking the breakwater. Your back to shore,
you cannot see that all the leaves, all
the late, glorious flowers
stretch toward you,
casting their shadows
away behind them.

Fall

Bushwhacking through niceties
as though everything is fine. As though
my throat is not seared with the futile thirst

for three quiet hours in your living room
as the late afternoon sun flops down
on the sofa, the bookshelf, its profligate spider plant.

It's a rare kind of light: forgiving enough
to lie naked under, my habit of cheeriness
piled beside me on the floor.

You can go on peeling carrots in the kitchen
as I listen to the floor creak under your shifting weight.
The autumn air will enter through the open window

and lay its cool hands on my desolate skin.
After some time you might make tea. Maybe
I will finally open a good book. This small time

might be all I really want of you. Yet to ask!
I would sooner hold my hand in a fire
and peel off the charred skin like a glove.

The Falls

The wind is building. Soon the forest will be bleak
as November and friendless, but today
it is still poplar golden, sunlight leaping down
through the fiery trees. I take you by the hand,
which is large and square, reliable
as a dictionary. We amble up the road through the fields,
into the woods and onto the ancient path
that follows the river past the fish pits to the cobbled lagoon.

Down the long descent into a canyon, silence
clings to us both as if we've just climbed
out of the river, cold and drenched. Beyond
the quiet of these woods, the rush
of the river is constant as breathing. It rises
as we draw near the steep gorge, funnelling
through the black rocks; reluctance
to speak grows too, as though
there is little to insist on, nothing
sure enough to shout out over the din of water.

At the valley bottom the land
spreads into a grove of cedars marked with long blazes
where the bark's been lifted off. In a thicket
of devil's club higher than our heads,
you stop to touch the last yellow leaves
clinging resolutely to the thorny stalks.
The pulse beats through your hand
and I realize, suddenly, how tightly I've gripped it
but already the trail has ended,
and you step out ahead onto the cobbled flats, walking on
towards the falls without looking back.
Our sounds are only those necessary
and inevitable: heartbeat, breath, worn rocks
clacking and faltering underfoot.

Firewood

Saturday, late September.
Sun the marrow of a bone-white sky.
Up at six and out, bumping up the mountain road
for the split, toss, stack. For this day: heft
of the maul swung behind and up
to its shoulders in birch. Birch's wood-clean scent.
For the weight of one cord then another
chopped and tossed, breath
of the maul's downward stroke, geese
filing up for the long passage south as you tip
each round, its harboured spiders
lurching from the terror of the empty sky.
Bend, pitch, next
piece by piece the day stacked up, split
at the ends by a wedge of dark
thought: this day, like its brothers, passing on
as the evening chill rolls into the small
of your back and your thoughts
cut into tomorrow, next week, next
spring—but in the swing of the upstroke
a pause: your stack, the sacrum summer sky,
its heartwood smell that is already
smoke rising through the cold
night: a surety.

Fog

Walking together through the aspen glen, more slowly
than we have ever walked. You lead me by the elbow because
it is some days now since my vision clouded over entirely.

How tenderly you describe the forest—sun dogs
capering through the autumn trees, a tangle of roots and toadstools
you so vigilantly keep me from falling over
with words like beautiful, golden, amazing! so that I will be content
and co-operate as you stoop to guide my foot
over yet another log. I can hear the patient kindness, the worry
softening the corners of your eyes. You urge me on. It will be all right.

But I trip and curse, despairing. Quit telling me that!
Nothing will be all right! How will I go on like this?
Trapped in this fog. I would run, jump in the car and tear off
but you are my only light. How can it be enough?
To be guided like this? Trusting you
to translate the world into words I can see.

A wind comes up with a sound like water—leaves
tugging loose and fluttering down all around.
You say nothing now, but I know by the chill in the air
that the sun has gone. Now we'll both struggle home
in the deepening dusk.

Nass

Tongue cut out, the land
splits along its fault line
and weeps flame. Downhill,
trees ignite like phosphorus.

The Nisga'a say it is the Earth
angry—though such ravaging
of mountains bespeaks
a more arduous pain.

The land tears open
the small of its back
where sorrow has lodged
like a block of shale. It spills

its infernal gut, its heart—
unseen, unknown—succumbing
to its incendiary craving
to strip off the scab

that staunched the secret
heat of its innards; its blind prophet
body shouting out in tongues
of flame as rain hisses in, scalded.

And now? The forest in ruins,
stony wasteland close behind.

Cranes

Dawn—almost. Going out to the barn with a pail
the sky is that same steel.
Again this morning my chest is a cold scrap yard
of broken, rusting things. It seems impossible

that they were ever useful. Picking my way through them
days ago, desperate for something functional, something
at least recognizable, I snagged a strand
of barbed wire. I've been lockjawed ever since.

Because everything departs as winter approaches. The leaves
cut off from what they'd thought was home. This morning
the first real snow glazes the mountains and I have squandered
a whole season to list upon list of tasks.

Now, midway across the yard, six sandhill cranes
pass overhead. They're so low I can hear their wings
skin the cold air. In unison they descend,
circling slowly, and alight on the drumlin in the far field.

Behind me over the trees, dawn ignites
the ragged clouds. The old door creaks open.
I bucket grain into the manger and draw the milking stool up.
Two streams of milk collide in the pail and the day

begins. In this season of endings, from this garden
of derelict tire rims, seized-up mower blades, there is so much
I would like to say. Leaning into this gentle, giving cow
she seems to me the natural condition of the world.

Grandfather

What became of the child who was good to you?
Remember how patient she was? It was you
who made her so, with your wondrous stories
of solar systems, of electrons, of the evolution of species.
I never write to you now, yet it would do us both good.
I would tell you of my life here. I would pen you
fifty fitful answers to each of my questions:

What is it to be wise? Will the beetles, the fishes,
forgive us their diminishing variety?
Why this constant going in circles?
Each answer will be new. By the time you receive it
you will have forgotten the question. Never mind.
We'll ask again: What was it to be patient?

I don't recall.
                    I've learned that the heart
in torment is at its most fecund. That it beats
towards tempests, listing under the weight
of too much cargo while half the hold always
wants filling. That it only rests long enough to feel
that such stillness goes nowhere, says nothing, hints
at surrender, at doldrums and a tired winding down.
So off it surges, restless as a river, bucking
any lasting peace because quiet, uneventful days

don't root in memory, which in the end moves out
like the tide. This is, at least, how it seems:
old happiness and heartbreak anchored fast
in you, though your mind is swept bare as the sand shore.

Negative Space

Again mid-winter. Sunset.
I return along the quay
toward a ragged stand of firs:
an ink-blot horizon. Backlit,

the steadfast trees
shaft through the ferrous sky
into the night beyond it.
Blink: their shape is the same

quick darkness, a familiar gap
in the intangible around them.
Though now they are no less mystery,
their blank silhouettes unrevealing.

I'd been seeing it backwards.
As if those trunks were the pillars
of a hollow sky. As if they would
stand surely as granite

as the wayward air rushed past.
Now the wind, impatient,
presses in and I step
into their flagging shadows.

Canyon

Almost spring, though
still too cold to pause long
amid the leafless aspen, the dry
pines on that broad open shelf
above the river.

                But we do

stop. Unexpectedly,
you reach for my hand

and I wake, choked, groping

for the fading joy of that small moment
in the cold blind sun
when all the weight of solitude
was only a small cloud scudding past. If only that

could be kept, instead of this
chill knowing, as you step back into the dream
and I fall out, that I am as much yours
as that sweep of broken rock
that leads the eye up a too-long canyon,
up the river just freed of ice,
over the basaltic ridges, the shadowed hollows
harbouring the last remnants of snow.

You glance back.
There is a minnow stranded on the road:
its small tail lifting, lifting again; its silver body
glinting under that quiet sun.

Speechless

Beside the river, the twilit path
offers up its talismans:
undergrowth beaded with last year's berries,
a sapsucker drumming overhead and,
under the first spectral violets,
a lichening hieroglyphic of vertebrae and ribs.

It seems someone should know the meaning
of these things, what fortunes or ill winds
they portend. Maybe pull together
a guidebook of sorts. Or a roadside crone
might cast her bones and read us
the semiotics of this land—

but there is no one here
for either end of this translation.
Shoulders hunched against the night, we're already
making for the car. The stars are only
pricks of light, and in my hands an old jawbone,
cracked and sublime, has lost the power of speech.

Fallen Leaves (Peace Valley Spring)

Half-hitched to yesterday, scoured out, smitten, you stood awash
    in an avalanche of sky—
    but root-bound, so you dreamt
avian: a rhumb line north, magnetic, or:
    smoke signals from Andromeda calling and calling you home.

The soul awake, though,
clunks.
More like alchemy
    reversed as it lopes off toward buckshot and sinkers and that last bright
    resting hole. But meanwhile,
you stood amid aspens barked up and blackened by frost. Lucid,
    the trees were articulate with wind
    and the ramshackle sunlight—how they leaned into it, greening!—
though the moose laid their thick teeth into that spring flourish,
into the bitter sap, that throb of…of? desire? fortitude? old
    habit?
In the snow, hoofprints
darken into pools
of shucked-off leaves. You lean in for their secrets,
and the secrets are
snow, old leaves.
    And, deeper:
    the cold ground. Knot of roots.
That is:
nothing
    you can use.

    (Yet here, just faintly,
    somewhere between
    gold dust and cast iron,
    your metallurgy
    sprouts leaves.)

Fish

A man is hewing a poplar log. He is alone,
his brother travelling the thirty miles to town
on horseback for supplies. He squares the log

with a broadaxe and dovetails the ends.
Hefting it into place, he regards his work,
props one end to smooth a closer joint. This house

he builds faces south to a field: rough,
stumped. Beyond the stumps are poplars, green
with early summer; beyond those, mountains.

Already the house is five logs high. He is strong
and quick. No neighbours for miles, he is also
isolated, and feels it. He doesn't imagine

the lilacs his sister will plant years from now,
her table whose length and generosity will make
a legend of this home. No, he sees himself

solitary, cloistered in dense bush, its silence,
compelled by his work but anxious, already,
to move on from here. In this, he is a steelhead

climbing doggedly upriver, engrossed in its own
story amid legions of other fish; its singular
tryst with the river, ascending a wilderness

of water that speaks in the glottal-stopped
dialect of shifting pebbles. The man hews this
testament into each log, imagining

the story he lives is his only. Yet his work,
his body belong to the land that receives them,
to the lineage trailing him like smoke.

Homesteading

Honey
on bread broken open,
bread just pulled from the blackened mouth
of this brick oven. Its breath scorches
the hair off your knuckles
as the children jostle
you, then the bread,
the honey, their fingers
thick with it, tapping sticky on the hot loaves
for you to crack open another
and spoon on the butter,
the honey, as steam
streams out and up in a rush
to the hawthorns overhead, their blossoms
sung through by air, the wind
of wings, such multitudes
of bees.

Wild Sage

A late spring hill.
Bones of karst
break through the wild sage.

Silent, a viper
thin and green as a reed
slips across the path.

Against the dust
its skin is so bright:
smooth jade

scales like little leaves
laid over its ribs.
It watches me.

Strong in me then:
the instinct to turn
back quickly; the desire

to kneel beside this snake
on the brilliant hillside,
in the wild soft sage,

to lay my hands
on its slender green length
and walk no further.

Nettles

Late winter: days bead up and trail,
stealing certainty. Like old raven
on the fence post scheming
to pluck day's coin from the sky,
then night's, I want to grasp
all the shining things that slide away.

Fearing sleep, I think of gannets:
intent on their fish, they plummet
one hundred feet, wide-eyed
as they strike the sea.

And the weak sun, the obliterating fog,
the river that in this shoulder season
could shrug and drop you through—
all insist *Why? What next? What
if?* This step onto a ribbon of ice—
backward glance cast to the safety
of shore—is hoarfrost's bloom
edging the cottonwood twigs.

But later, crossing Hagwilget Canyon
at sunset, mid-May, my only wish
is to slip for a moment into the skin
of those fine-boned aspens
spooning the spring wind. The light
slides down the throat of the canyon, over
the shoulders of rock
to the river, so far below the bridge
I can ignore what it has to say.
But I can't slow it, can't
stop it, and at last

June arrives; my heart, like the new green,
can't contain itself.
                    Other times
of the year knowledge we arrive at comes slowly,
ponderously, hurting us
all the way. But by June, green
is no longer incremental. It comes barrelling full tilt
across a field, greeting me the way the farm dog does,
leaping up all around. And an old friend would say—bare-handed
in the kitchen, arms full of nettles—that there is no pain here,
just a tingling: the sense of being
                    fully alive

in this world that again invites us
to leave the husks of our old selves
clinging to the rocks along the riverbank
as we emerge translucent
and climb into the morning light.

Seven Songs for Spatsizi

On the stones beside the lake,
gazing into the cold, black eye of it.

Let go the stones underfoot,
the stout spruce handholds:
this alpine water an ablution.

To lie down on ground thickly printed
with the passage of animals is to wake

to a dream of two moose.
Though it is silent, this waking, they pause

in their walking, in the moonlit scrub willows,
and turn their unhurried gaze toward it.

And when, walking   through the enormous and solitary land,
you grow hungry for company, you will find it underfoot: this trail

the companionship of moose, of black bears, caribou and goats—
unseen but sharing, for a small time, the same journey.

The creek, also, accompanied you,
though at times you feared it might drown

bush noises of approaching bears. Now,
two days up, it's dwindled to a silent pond;

a pack-horse trail curves alongside
and away into diminishing spruce.

Wind rattles down the pass
and with it ragged clouds, rain.

Everywhere here, grief: a July snow
on the crowberries and a lone bleached antler.

There is always
death. All the way, walking alongside,

it keeps pace.

It is above the lake, at the edge of the plateau,
where the southwest is a sawtooth range, the northeast
a sweep of highland honed smooth as a rib,
that the sky—rain-smudged, cantering—is loudest,

burnishing the callous ground and its five o'clock
scrub-grass shadow. A hawk shoulders in: headlong,
headstrong, it dips to follow the sine-curved land,
the smooth land, exigent land, unadorned and edgeless as the sea.

How to speak
to this wind running past

to join the water gathering
at the foot of the mountain?

Long ago, a boulder—
large as a house—

fell from the cliff high above.
Mossy, it rests now amid the trees.

On reaching the river that gleams broadly
in the nostalgic evening, drop
all gear, all clothing and descend the last slope
to the riverbank, cross its black sand

and walk out of midsummer's miasma
of insects into the icy stream. Take care
lest it take you, for, like the mountains,
it is stronger than it knows and cannot stop flowing.

Swadeshi

I would urge that Swadeshi is the only doctrine
consistent with the law of humility and love.
~ Mahatma Gandhi

And because words, if they were possible at all,
were illegitimate, tawdry,
I spoke to you in yarns.

That is, I knelt in the leafless orchard
where the ewes grazed in hope of some final windfall
apple nestled in the last grass. It was wrong of me,
with winter coming, to hold her tight against me and lay in
with the old shears, but there was ice in the fall air, a loneliness.
And she was so gentle, her fine-boned legs
held stiffly in the air in front of her, a sort of resigned serenity
in her quiet breath. She made no sound;
it was quiet except for the grate and snip of heavy shears,
the almost indiscernible swish in the cropped grass as the other sheep
moved through it, watching me, ruminating intensely on this unexpected
disturbance. The fleece fell away cleanly as she lurched up
and turned briefly to regard me with her arcane gaze
then trotted off to her companions.
I sank my fingers into the softness she'd left: a dense heap of smoke
musty with lanolin that stung the cracks in my hands.
It came into my arms. Thus began our conversation.

Hour on hour to tease it apart, to pull the burrs and twigs that worried it.
I built a fire in the old brick hearth and sat in the threadbare armchair,
a fog of open wool gathering at my ankles. Each hour I rose
to stir or feed the fire, crouching with a poker
in the tall smudge of wool as the growing flames
stroked the wood then slowly climbed into it and held there, glowing.

Then other tasks intruded and it was some days
before I spoke to you again. This time over a warm bath,
the wool steeping, the water stained barnyard brown. There was nothing
pleasant about that wet-sheep smell as I plunged my wrinkled hands in.
It's just part of it, I told you, and hauled the soaked and reeking fleece out
as gently as I was able. A layer of filth covered the tub when the water ran out.
Just part of it. I washed it down and filled the tub again.
Wet wool wants to mat and moving it is a slow negotiation: no sudden
movements or the work so far is lost. I put it in to rinse
and the wool bloomed open in the liquid warmth. I said,
how about a cup of coffee?

So I brewed a pot and we sat drinking it black as the wool dried on a rack
between us and the fire. Neither of us spoke. Mostly because
I couldn't imagine what you would have said. Maybe that this project
was eminently foolish. How many days work for a little warmth?
Pre-empting you, I said it would be worth it. That this blanket
would be the softest and loftiest you'd ever felt. That, holding it,
you would feel in the heft of the weave this work, its meaning.
You didn't reply. You doubted it. Or maybe you were moved
that I would go to all this trouble. I liked to think so.
But you might actually have found me ridiculous.

In fact, I was sure of it. I was ridiculous as I took the pearly
drifts of clean, dry wool in my hands. As I heaped them
onto the combs and raked them straight. Sad and foolish,
I worked a long snake of wool through the hole in the clamshell diz and it coiled
beside me on the floor. Over and over: piling the combs, raking the wool,
pulling the sliver through. The mound spread over my feet.
You weren't there. I was alone in despair at the weight
of the work, at the magnitude of indifference that makes this work
useless. There are blankets at the store and you had one already.
You were warm enough. I was redundant.

Resigned, I came to the spinning wheel and thought
not of you but of Gandhi at his charkha. How such kind hands
and simple work could change everything.
Three days, he'd said, eight hours each. That will give you yarn for a year.

I worked the treadle and watched the loose strand become yarn in my hands.
There's a finality in it, in working those wisps into a steel line. The softness goes.
It becomes an in-between thing, a sad thing heavy with desire
to be unspooled, to be worn. That yarn a timeline,
twenty four hours long. A coiled horizon, a frontier. Or a fenceline—the way
I've cordoned myself off with this nonsensical effort. What is it in the end
but two strands of aloneness plied double thick?

It was deep winter; ice etched across the old windowpanes.
Snow burdened the spruces and bent the willow across the paths.
I went out to gather lichen. The thought of you came too.
I showed you the foliose type that dyes a rich brown; *Usnea* for green.
You said you were sorry to have put me to such trouble.

I was silent. How to tell you
that in truth it was no trouble? That thinking of you
made me glad.

So many soft hues in the skeins of yarn hung drying
on broomsticks laid across the backs of chairs.
Silvery greens, grey browns. They waited
as new marsh grass waits while the snow grows patchy.

Bird's-eye twill, six hundred ends. So intricate was the work
that its details crowded out all else. The old beech loom
stood patient as an aging draft horse
as I moved around and over it, climbing onto its hefty frame
to straighten all the harnesses and check the lines.
Six hundred threads to keep untangled, to align, one by one in orderly sequence,
from the back beam through six hundred heddles, six hundred
separate slots in the reed. By the time I had finished and knotted them all down
and wrapped the warp onto the front beam at the ready
I was like an old woman: my back
would not straighten, a web of tense lines
had deepened at the corners of my eyes.
But I slid under the loom like a mechanic
to tie up the treadles in the last hour before midnight.

Then, the loom threaded, the warp immaculate, I saw again
the nature of our conversation:
all the threads ran one way.

But when I began to toss the shuttle, as the cloth grew
under my hands, colloquy blossomed into cacophony. The cast-iron
cranks and gears on the old loom, the brake and the beater
clapped and sang like a gospel choir. Spring meltwater
light flooded the room and drenched all the living
colours in the wool. Above the raucous chicken yard
and the looping barn swallows, the sun climbed steadily.
The near mountains glistened.

I worked clear through the frog-song night and when dawn came
I cut it free. Unfurled it from the loom. It billowed out
the way a sail climbs a mast in a few quick halyard pulls,
snapping open in the morning light—that quick instant
the story of our kind. Ingenious capture. The way into a whole
civilization and its ugly deceits. But there is also a way
of being careful. Here, spread in soft folds across the floor:
only the labour of my own attentive hands.

This entwinement of yarn:
all the words that lived in me, the finest
I could craft. I gave them to you.

You laid the gift aside and took my open hands. Left, right
you kissed the inside of each wrist.
There, where the skin is thinnest.

You took your gift.
It held you all night.

NOTES

The epigraph of "Rainstorm" is an anonymous translation of a well-known passage from the 1894 novel *Le Lys Rouge*, by Anatole France.

"Una via dove mi specchio" is the title of a poem in the collection *Trieste e una donna* by Umberto Saba, Arnoldo Mondadori Editore. The epigraph by Rilke is taken from the poem *"Herbsttag"* (*The Selected Poetry of Rainer Maria Rilke*, translated by Stephen Mitchell, Random House).

9.8 m/s^2 (9.8 metres per second squared) is the rate of acceleration due to gravity.

The Greek physician Dioskorides (ca. 40 – ca. 90) worked as a surgeon with the Roman army throughout the Roman Empire. During this time, he compiled *De Materia Medica*, which remained the authoritative guide to medicinal plants for over 1500 years. *Nardos* and *kyklaminos* are valerian and cyclamen.

The epigraph of "Cuttlefish Bone" is from *"Ossi di Sepia"* by Eugenio Montale (*Collected Poems 1920-1954*, edited by Jonathan Galassi, Farrar Straus and Giroux).

The epigraph of "Wild Sage" by Antoine St. Exupery is taken from his 1943 novella *Le Petit Prince* (Editions Gallimard).

"Swadeshi" is the principle espoused by Mahatma Gandhi that service to one's immediate neighbours results in service to humanity. The epigraph is taken from Gandhi's writings.

ACKNOWLEDGEMENTS

Earlier versions of these poems were published in *The Malahat Review, Contemporary Verse II, The Antigonish Review, Room, The New Quarterly, The Fiddlehead, Prairie Fire, Qwerty* and *Geez.* Many thanks to the editors of these publications for their support, as well as to those of other publications who gave their time and attention to the pieces I sent them.

A collection of these poems was awarded the RBC Bronwen Wallace Award for Emerging Writers from the Writers' Trust of Canada. Thanks to everyone involved in administering this award (particularly James Davies and Carolyn Smart) for their support, without which this book would likely still be a sheaf of papers in a drawer.

The poem "Wokkpash" was broadcast on CBC's *As it Happens* and for this special thanks go to Carol Off, Barbara Budd and everyone else who welcomed my impromptu visit to the studio.

Thanks also to Jan Zwicky and Tim Lilburn for their guidance and wisdom at the Banff Centre and during the In the Field program.

Particular gratitude is due to the production team at Brick Books and to Elizabeth Philips who brought her insight, attention and patience to the editorial process.

I am deeply grateful to family and friends who have in many ways contributed to the poems in this book. In particular, I would like to thank Jonathan, Jenny, Roberta and Enzo and, of course, Tim and Jane for their kindness, encouragement and support over the years.

"Insects in Lamplight After Rain" is for my friend Abdul Sunshine Jalloh.

Emily McGiffin's poetry was awarded the 2008 Bronwen Wallace Award for Emerging Writers from the Writers' Trust of Canada and was a finalist for the CBC Literary Awards in 2004 and 2005. She lives in northwest BC.